THE BOOK
OF LIGHT

THE BOOK
OF LIGHT

LUCILLE
CLIFTON

COPPER CANYON PRESS

Poems in this collection have appeared in *American Poetry Review*, *Belle Lettres*, *Kenyon Review*, *Quarry West*, and *Yankee Magazine*.

Publication of this book is supported by a grant from the National Endowment for the Arts and a grant from the Lannan Foundation. Additional support to Copper Canyon Press has been provided by the Andrew W. Mellon Foundation, the Lila Wallace-Reader's Digest Fund, and the Washington State Arts Commission. Copper Canyon Press is in residence with Centrum at Fort Worden State Park.

Library of Congress Cataloging-in-Publication Data

Clifton, Lucille, 1936–
        The book of light : poems / by Lucille Clifton.
            p.   cm.
        ISBN 1-55659-051-2 : $21.00. – ISBN 1-55659-052-0 (pbk.) : $11.00
        I. Title.
PS3553.L45B66   1993
811'.54 – d c 2 0   92-40537

COPPER CANYON PRESS
Post Office Box 271
Port Townsend, Washington 98368

TABLE OF CONTENTS

7 : LIGHT

reflection

lightning bolt

splendor

for Kathy

you sister david

LIGHT

ray

stream

gleam

beam

sun

glow

flicker

shine

lucid

spark

scintilla

flash

blaze

flame

fire

serene

luciferous

lightning bolt

luster

shimmer

glisten

gloss

brightness

brilliance

splendor

sheen

dazzle

sparkle
luminous
reflection
kindle
illuminate
brighten
glorious
radiate
radiant
splendid
clarify
clear

ROGET'S THESAURUS

reflection

climbing

a woman precedes me up the long rope,
her dangling braids the color of rain.
maybe i should have had braids.
maybe i should have kept the body i started,
slim and possible as a boy's bone.
maybe i should have wanted less.
maybe i should have ignored the bowl in me
burning to be filled.
maybe i should have wanted less.
the woman passes the notch in the rope
marked Sixty.   i rise toward it, struggling,
hand over hungry hand.

june 20

i will be born in one week
to a frowned forehead of a woman
and a man whose fingers will itch
to enter me. she will crochet
a dress for me of silver
and he will carry me in it.
they will do for each other
all that they can
but it will not be enough.
none of us know that we will not
smile again for years,
that she will not live long.
in one week i will emerge face first
into their temporary joy.

daughters

woman who shines at the head
of my grandmother's bed,
brilliant woman, i like to think
you whispered into her ear
instructions. i like to think
you are the oddness in us,
you are the arrow
that pierced our plain skin
and made us fancy women;
my wild witch gran, my magic mama,
and even these gaudy girls.
i like to think you gave us
extraordinary power and to
protect us, you became the name
we were cautioned to forget.
it is enough,
you must have murmured,
to remember that i was
and that you are. woman, i am
lucille, which stands for light,
daughter of thelma, daughter
of georgia, daughter of
dazzling you.

sam

if he could have kept
the sky in his dark hand
he would have pulled it down
and held it.
it would have called him lord
as did the skinny women
in virginia. if he
could have gone to school
he would have learned to write
his story and not live it.
if he could have done better
he would have. oh stars
and stripes forever,
what did you do to my father?

my lost father

see where he moves
he leaves a wake of tears
see in the path of his going
the banners of regret
see just above him the cloud
of welcome   see him rise
see him enter the company
of husbands   fathers   sons

thel

was my first landscape,
red brown as the clay
of her georgia.
sweet attic of a woman,
repository of old songs.
there was such music in her;
she would sit, shy as a wren
humming alone and lonely
amid broken promises,
amid the sweet broken bodies
of birds.

imagining bear

for alonzo moore sr.

imagine him too tall and too wide
for the entrance into parlors

imagine his hide gruff, the hair on him
grizzled even to his own hand

imagine his odor surrounding him,
rank and bittersweet as bark

imagine him lumbering as he moves
imagine his growl filling the wind

give him an old guitar
give him a bottle of booze

imagine his children laughing; papa   papa
imagine his wife sighing; oh lonnie

imagine him singing, imagine his granddaughter
remembering him in poems

c.c. rider

who is that running away
with my life? who is that
black horse, who is that rider
dressed like my sons, braided
like my daughters? who is that
georgia woman, who is that
virginia man, who is that light-eyed
stranger not looking back?
who is that hollow woman? who am i?
see see rider, see what you have done.

11/10 again

some say the radiance around the body
can be seen by eyes latticed against
all light but the particular. they say
you can notice something rise
from the houseboat of the body
wearing the body's face,
and that you can feel the presence
of a possible otherwhere.
not mystical, they say, but human,
human to lift away from the arms that
try to hold you (as you did then)
and, brilliance magnified,
circle beyond the ironwork
encasing your human heart.

she lived

after he died
what really happened is
she watched the days
bundle into thousands,
watched every act become
the history of others,
every bed more
narrow,
but even as the eyes of lovers
strained toward the milky young
she walked away
from the hole in the ground
deciding to live.   and she lived.

for roddy

i am imagining this of you,
turned away from breath
as you turned from my body,
refusing to defile what you adored;
i am imagining rejuvenated bones
rising from the dead floor where
they found you, rising and running
back into the life you loved,
dancing as you would dance
toward me, wherever, whose ever i am.

them and us

something in their psyche insists on elvis
slouching into markets, his great collar
high around his great head, his sideburns
extravagant, elvis, still swiveling those
negro hips. something needs to know

that even death, the most faithful manager
can be persuaded to give way
before real talent, that it is possible
to triumph forever on a timeless stage
surrounded by lovers giving the kid a hand.

we have so many gone. history
has taught us much about fame and its
inevitable tomorrow. we ride the subways
home from the picture show, sure about
death and elvis, but watching for marvin gaye.

the women you are accustomed to

wearing that same black dress,
their lips and asses tight,
their bronzed hair set in perfect place;
these women gathered in my dream
to talk their usual talk,
their conversation spiked with the names
of avenues in France.

and when i asked them what the hell,
they shook their marble heads
and walked erect out of my sleep,
back into a town which knows
all there is to know
about the cold outside, while i relaxed
and thought of you,
your burning blood, your dancing tongue.

song at midnight

. . . do not
send me out
among strangers
                    — Sonia Sanchez

brothers,
this big woman
carries much sweetness
in the folds of her flesh.
her hair
is white with wonderful.
she is
rounder than the moon
and far more faithful.
brothers,
who will hold her,
who will find her beautiful
if you do not?

won't you celebrate with me
what i have shaped into
a kind of life? i had no model.
born in babylon
both nonwhite and woman
what did i see to be except myself?
i made it up
here on this bridge between
starshine and clay,
my one hand holding tight
my other hand; come celebrate
with me that everyday
something has tried to kill me
and has failed.

lightning bolt

it was a dream

in which my greater self
rose up before me
accusing me of my life
with her extra finger
whirling in a gyre of rage
at what my days had come to.
what,
i pleaded with her, could i do,
oh what could i have done?
and she twisted her wild hair
and sparked her wild eyes
and screamed as long as
i could hear her
This.   This.   This.

*   *   *

each morning i pull myself
out of despair

from a night of coals and a tongue
blistered with smiling

the step past the mother bed
is a high step

the walk through the widow's door
is a long walk

and who are these voices calling
from every mirrored thing

say it coward say it

here yet be dragons

so many languages have fallen
off of the edge of the world
into the dragon's mouth. some

where there be monsters whose teeth
are sharp and sparkle with lost

people. lost poems. who
among us can imagine ourselves
unimagined? who

among us can speak with so fragile
tongue and remain proud?

the yeti poet returns to his village to tell his story

...found myself wondering
if i had entered
the valley of shadow

found myself wandering
a shrunken world
of hairless men

oh the pouches
they close themselves into
at night   oh the thin
paps of their women

i turned from the click
of their spirit-catching box
the boom of their long stick

and made my way back
to this wilderness
where we know where we are
what we are

crabbing

(the poet crab speaks)

pulling
into their pots
our wives
our hapless children.
crabbing
they smile, meaning us
i imagine,
though our name
is our best secret.
this forward moving
fingered thing
inedible
even to itself,
how can it understand
the sweet sacred meat
of others?

the earth is a living thing

is a black shambling bear
ruffling its wild back and tossing
mountains into the sea

is a black hawk circling
the burying ground circling the bones
picked clean and discarded

is a fish black blind in the belly of water
is a diamond blind in the black belly of coal

is a black and living thing
is a favorite child
of the universe
feel her rolling her hand
in its kinky hair
feel her brushing it clean

move

On May 13, 1985 Wilson Goode, Philadelphia's first Black mayor, authorized
the bombing of 6221 Osage Avenue after the complaints of neighbors, also
Black, about the Afrocentric back-to-nature group headquartered there and
calling itself Move. All the members of the group wore dreadlocks and had taken
the surname Africa. In the bombing eleven people, including children, were
killed and sixty-one homes in the neighborhood were destroyed.

they had begun to whisper
among themselves   hesitant
to be branded neighbor to the wild
haired women the naked children
reclaiming a continent
away

move

he hesitated
then turned his smoky finger
toward africa toward the house
he might have lived in might have
owned or saved had he not turned
away

move

the helicopter rose at the command
higher at first then hesitating
then turning toward the center

of its own town only a neighborhood
away

move

she cried as the child stood
hesitant in the last clear sky
he would ever see   the last
before the whirling blades the whirling smoke
and sharp debris carried all clarity
away

move

if you live in a mind
that would destroy itself
to comfort itself
if you would stand fire
rather than difference
do not hesitate
move
away

samson predicts from gaza
the philadelphia fire

for ramona africa, survivor

it will be your hair
ramona africa
they will come for you
they will bring fire
they will empty your eyes
of everything you love
your hair will writhe
and hiss on your shoulder
they will order you
to give it up   if you do
you will bring the temple down
if you do not   they will

january 1991

they have sent our boy
to muffle himself
in the sand. our son
who has worshipped skin,
pale and visible as heaven,
all his life,
who has practiced the actual
name of God,
who knows himself to be
the very photograph of Adam.
yes, our best boy is there
with his bright-eyed sister,
both of them waiting in dunes
distant as Mars
to shutter the dark veiled lids
of not our kind.
they, who are not us, they have
no life we recognize,
no heaven we can care about,
no word for God we can pronounce.
we do not know them,
do not want to know them,
do not want this lying at night
all over the bare stone county
dreaming of desert for the first time
and of death and our boy and his sister
and them and us.

dear jesse helms,

something is happening.
something obscene.

in the night sky
the stars are bursting

into flame. thousands
and thousands of lights

are pouring down onto
the children of allah,

and jesse,

the smart bombs do not recognize
the babies. something

is happening obscene.

they are shrouding words so that
families cannot find them.

civilian deaths have become
collateral damage, bullets

are anti-personnel. jesse,
the fear is anti-personnel.

jesse, the hate is anti-personnel.
jesse, the war is anti-personnel,

and something awful is happening.
something obscene.

if i should

to clark kent

enter the darkest room
in my house and speak
with my own voice, at last,
about its awful furniture,
pulling apart the covering
over the dusty bodies; the randy
father, the husband holding ice
in his hand like a blessing,
the mother bleeding into herself
and the small imploding girl,
i say if i should walk into
that web, who will come flying
after me, leaping tall buildings?
you?

further note to clark

do you know how hard this is for me?
do you know what you're asking?

what i can promise to be is water,
water plain and direct as Niagara.
unsparing of myself, unsparing of
the cliff i batter, but also unsparing
of you, tourist. the question for me is
how long can i cling to this edge?
the question for you is
what have you ever traveled toward
more than your own safety?

begin here

in the dark
where the girl is
sleeping
begin with a shadow
rising on the wall
no
begin with a spear
of salt like a tongue
no
begin with a swollen
horn   or finger
no
no   begin here
something in the girl
is wakening   some
thing in the girl
is falling
deeper and deeper
asleep

night vision

the girl fits her body in
to the space between the bed
and the wall. she is a stalk,
exhausted. she will do some
thing with this. she will
surround these bones with flesh.
she will cultivate night vision.
she will train her tongue
to lie still in her mouth and listen.
the girl slips into sleep.
her dream is red and raging.
she will remember
to build something human with it.

fury

remember this.
she is standing by
the furnace.
the coals
glisten like rubies.
her hand is crying.
her hand is clutching
a sheaf of papers.
poems.
she gives them up.
they burn
jewels into jewels.
her eyes are animals.
each hank of her hair
is a serpent's obedient
wife.
she will never recover.
remember. there is nothing
you will not bear
for this woman's sake.

cigarettes

my father burned us all. ash
fell from his hand onto our beds,
onto our tables and chairs.
ours was the roof the sirens
rushed to at night
mistaking the glow of his pain
for flame. nothing is burning here,
my father would laugh, ignoring
my charred pillow, ignoring his own
smoldering halls.

final note to clark

they had it wrong,
the old comics.
you are only clark kent
after all. oh,
mild mannered mister,
why did i think you could fix it?
how you must have wondered
to see me taking chances,
dancing on the edge of words,
pointing out the bad guys,
dreaming your x-ray vision
could see the beauty in me.
what did i expect? what
did i hope for? we are who we are,
two faithful readers,
not wonder woman and not superman.

note, passed to superman

sweet jesus, superman,
if i had seen you
dressed in your blue suit
i would have known you.
maybe that choirboy clark
can stand around
listening to stories
but not you, not with
metropolis to save
and every crook in town
filthy with kryptonite.
lord, man of steel,
i understand the cape,
the leggings, the whole
ball of wax.
you can trust me,
there is no planet stranger
than the one i'm from.

*   *   *

love the human
             – Gary Snyder

the rough weight of it
scarring its own back
the dirt under the fingernails
the bloody cock   love
the thin line secting the belly
the small gatherings
gathered in sorrow or joy
love the silences
love the terrible noise
love the stink of it
love it all   love
even the improbable foot   even
the surprised and ungrateful eye

splendor

seeker of visions

what does this mean
to see walking men
wrapped in the color of death,
to hear from their tongue
such difficult syllables?
are they the spirits
of our hope
or the pale ghosts of our future?
who will believe the red road
will not run on forever?
who will believe
a tribe of ice might live
and we might not?

columbus day '91

*   *   *

Nothing is told us about Sisyphus in the underworld.
                                    – Albert Camus

nothing about the moment
just after the ball fits itself
into the bottom of the hill
and the world is suspended
and i become king of this country
all imps and imposters watching
me,
waiting me, and i decide, i decide
whether or not i will allow
this myth to live. i slide
myself down. demons restoke the
fire.
i push my shoulder into the round
world and taste in my mouth
how sweet power is, the story
gods never tell.

atlas

i am used to the heft of it
sitting against my rib,
used to the ridges of forest,
used to the way my thumb
slips into the sea as i pull
it tight. something is sweet
in the thick odor of flesh
burning and sweating and bearing young.
i have learned to carry it
the way a poor man learns
to carry everything.

sarah's promise

who understands better than i
the hunger in old bones
for a son? so here we are,
abraham with his faith
and i my fury. jehovah,
i march into the thicket
of your need and promise you
the children of young women,
yours for a thousand years.
their faith will send them to you,
docile as abraham. now,
speak to my husband.
spare me my one good boy.

naomi watches as ruth sleeps

she clings to me
like a shadow
when all that i wish
is to sit alone
longing for my husband,
my sons.
she has promised
to follow me,
to become me
if i allow it.
i am leading her
to boaz country.
he will find her beautiful
and place her among
his concubines.
jehovah willing
i can grieve in peace.

cain

so this is what it means
to be an old man;
every member of my body
limp and unsatisfied,
father to sons who never knew
my father, husband to the
sister of the east,
and all night, in the rocky
land of nod,
listening to the thunderous
roll of voices,
unable to tell them where
my brother is.

leda 1

there is nothing luminous
about this.
they took my children.
i live alone in the backside
of the village.
my mother moved
to another town. my father
follows me around the well,
his thick lips slavering,
and at night my dreams are full
of the cursing of me
fucking god fucking me.

leda 2

a note on visitations

sometimes another star chooses.
the ones coming in from the east
are dagger-fingered men,
princes of no known kingdom.
the animals are raised up in their stalls
battering the stable door.
sometimes it all goes badly;
the inn is strewn with feathers,
the old husband suspicious,
and the fur between her thighs
is the only shining thing.

leda 3

a personal note (re: visitations)

always pyrotechnics;
stars spinning into phalluses
of light, serpents promising
sweetness, their forked tongues
thick and erect, patriarchs of bird
exposing themselves in the air.
this skin is sick with loneliness.
You want what a man wants,
next time come as a man
or don't come.

far memory

a poem in seven parts

1
convent

my knees recall the pockets
worn into the stone floor,
my hands, tracing against the wall
their original name, remember
the cold brush of brick, and the smell
of the brick powdery and wet
and the light finding its way in
through the high bars.

and also the sisters singing
at matins, their sweet music
the voice of the universe at peace
and the candles their light the light
at the beginning of creation
and the wonderful simplicity of prayer
smooth along the wooden beads
and certainly attended.

2
someone inside me remembers

that my knees must be hidden away
that my hair must be shorn
so that vanity will not test me
that my fingers are places of prayer
and are holy   that my body is promised
to something more certain
than myself

3
again

born in the year of war
on the day of perpetual help.

come from the house
of stillness
through the soft gate
of a silent mother.

come to a betraying father.
come to a husband who would one day
rise and enter a holy house.

come to wrestle with you again,
passion, old disobedient friend,
through the secular days and nights
of another life.

4
trying to understand this life

who did i fail, who
did i cease to protect
that i should wake each morning
facing the cold north?

perhaps there is a cart
somewhere in history
of children crying "sister
save us" as she walks away.

the woman walks into my dreams
dragging her old habit.
i turn from her, shivering,
to begin another afternoon
of rescue, rescue.

5
sinnerman

horizontal one evening
on the cold stone,
my cross burning into
my breast, did i dream
through my veil
of his fingers digging
and is this the dream
again, him, collarless
over me, calling me back
to the stones of this world
and my own whispered
hosanna?

6
karma

the habit is heavy.
you feel its weight
pulling around your ankles
for a hundred years.

the broken vows
hang against your breasts,
each bead a word
that beats you.

even now
to hear the words
defend
protect
goodbye
lost or
alone
is to be washed in sorrow.

and in this life
there is no retreat
no sanctuary
no whole abiding
sister.

7
gloria mundi

so knowing,
what is known?
that we carry our baggage
in our cupped hands
when we burst through
the waters of our mother.
that some are born
and some are brought
to the glory of this world.
that it is more difficult
than faith
to serve only one calling
one commitment
one devotion
in one life.

brothers

(being a conversation in eight poems between an aged Lucifer and God,
though only Lucifer is heard. The time is long after.)

1
invitation

come coil with me
here in creation's bed
among the twigs and ribbons
of the past. i have grown old
remembering this garden,
the hum of the great cats
moving into language, the sweet
fume of the man's rib
as it rose up and began to walk.
it was all glory then,
the winged creatures leaping
like angels, the oceans claiming
their own. let us rest here a time
like two old brothers
who watched it happen and wondered
what it meant.

2
how great Thou art

listen, You are beyond
even Your own understanding.
that rib and rain and clay
in all its pride,
its unsteady dominion,
is not what You believed
You were,
but it is what You are;
in Your own image as some
lexicographer supposed.
the face, both he and she,
the odd ambition, the desire
to reach beyond the stars
is You. all You, all You
the loneliness, the perfect
imperfection.

3
as for myself

less snake than angel
less angel than man
how come i to this
serpent's understanding?
watching creation from
a hood of leaves
i have foreseen the evening
of the world.
as sure as she,
the breast of Yourself
separated out and made to bear,
as sure as her returning,
i too am blessed with
the one gift you cherish;
to feel the living move in me
and to be unafraid.

4
in my own defense

what could i choose
but to slide along behind them,
they whose only sin
was being their father's children?
as they stood with their backs
to the garden,
a new and terrible luster
burning their eyes,
only You could have called
their ineffable names,
only in their fever
could they have failed to hear.

5
the road led from delight

into delight. into the sharp
edge of seasons, into the sweet
puff of bread baking, the warm
vale of sheet and sweat after love,
the tinny newborn cry of calf
and cormorant and humankind.
and pain, of course,
always there was some bleeding,
but forbid me not
my meditation on the outer world
before the rest of it, before
the bruising of his heel, my head,
and so forth.

6
"the silence of God is God."
　　　　　– Carolyn Forché

tell me, tell us why
in the confusion of a mountain
of babies stacked like cordwood,
of limbs walking away from each other,
of tongues bitten through
by the language of assault,
tell me, tell us why
You neither raised Your hand
nor turned away, tell us why
You watched the excommunication of
that world and You said nothing.

7
still there is mercy, there is grace

how otherwise
could i have come to this
marble spinning in space
propelled by the great
thumb of the universe?
how otherwise
could the two roads
of this tongue
converge into a single
certitude?
how otherwise
could i, a sleek old
traveler,
curl one day safe and still
beside You
at Your feet, perhaps,
but, amen, Yours.

8
". . . . . is God."

so.
having no need to speak
You sent Your tongue
splintered into angels.
even i,
with my little piece of it
have said too much.
to ask You to explain
is to deny You.
before the word
You were.
You kiss my brother mouth.
the rest is silence.

about the poet

Lucille Clifton was born in Depew, New York in 1936, and edu-
cated at the State University of New York at Fredonia and at
Howard University. Her awards include the Juniper Prize for
Poetry, two nominations for the Pulitzer Prize in poetry, an
Emmy Award from the American Academy of Television Arts and
Sciences, and two fellowships from the National Endowment
for the Arts. She has taught at the University of California at Santa
Cruz and American University in Washington, D.C. and is presently
Distinguished Professor of Humanities at St. Marys College of
Maryland.